THE POTION FOR EMOTION

Tina Mathurin

Anna,

Thank you for all
your help & support.

Your talkative colleague.

Tina xx

ARTHUR H. STOCKWELL LTD.
Torrs Park Ilfracombe Devon
Established 1898
www.ahstockwell.co.uk

First published in Great Britain, 2007

British Library Cataloguing-in-Publication Data.
A catalogue record for this book is available from the British Library.

ISBN 978-0-7223-3828-5
Printed in Great Britain by
Arthur H. Stockwell Ltd.
Torrs Park Ilfracombe
Devon

I would just like to thank:
My first husband, Nick, for keeping me at home for so long, alone. This gave me the space and time I needed. My second husband, John, for giving me the initial encouragement to carry on. My present and last husband, Michael, for giving me a good balance of each. And finally, my children, Ants, Steve, Sam and Chops, who, no matter what, have inspired a lot of my thoughts.

I've voiced my opinions, more than just a word or two.
I will myself to care no matter what.
It's much easier though, to say than do.

Contents

Since When?

Since when did
The young lamb I married turn into a cow-like ewe?
Since when did
The fresh young piglet change to this pot-bellied hog?
Since when did
I lose my affectionately cute puppy dog?
Since when did
I marry the sex kitten, not the fat cat who ate all the cream?
Since when did
Her hourglass figure become the pear-shaped nightmarish dream?
Since when have
I passed a mirror and smiled 'cos I'm pleased to see me?
Since when did
My prospects of pulling a bird suddenly become so bleak?
Since when was
I content to have sex routinely just once a week?
Since when did
I voice my opinion?
Since when have
I gone on like a clucky old hen?
Since when did
I lose a mind of my own?
Made a choice, a decision?
Since When?

Westray Days

It's lonely in this empty house.
The breeze blows through the trees.
I'm waiting for you to come home,
But hurry, won't you, please.

My patience now is wearing.
The baby cries all day.
He throws his toys upon the floor.
Come home, please, now I pray.

I sit in the rocking chair.
I watch the time go by.
At the door I stare and stare.
You're the one main reason why.

I can't believe my eyes now.
You walk in through the door.
The answer to my loneliness;
The one I've waited for.

I expect words like, "I love you."
Or, "Hi, love, how was your day?"
But, it's "Go and put the kettle on;"
The very same as yesterday.

Stay young, free and single.
Carefree, ***not in love***.
Make the most of life while you still can
And ***don't depend on love!***

It's Sad

It's sad to watch her just sit.
Mind willing, the body wants out of it.
Life is so cruel.
Why, when the body is old, do the legs give way?
She needs them more now, in every way.
She's always been my kindred spirit.
She taught me, ironically, strength of will.
Life goes on, we tough it out.
She cares about me utmost still.
Is it not bad enough to lose pride and dignity?
It's in the least a shameful pity.
When others neglect
It brings about a duo effect.
Old age being a titanic strife,
Unable to keep up in the sea of life.
Autumn of life, like leaves we fall back down,
Miss the life raft, then we drown.

Age Concern

Age concern applies to us all.
We too will be old, no hair at all.
Memory loss, lack of respect.
Demoralised, talked down to, neglect.
They feel inside as young as we do.
The rattly old frame doesn't work like it used to.
They're disabled really, that's about all.
Living with the fear of the one fatal fall.
Thinking that every day could just be their last.
All joy and loved ones remain in the past.
"Oh, just to go back,"
They regretfully cry,
To their youth.
"Not let a day go by
Without a hug or a smile."
Those were the days
When their lives were worthwhile.

Roots

The grass may be greener on the other side
But, this is ***our*** grass,
Our roots are here.
If we leave we carry with us our tears.

Tears of joy and of sorrow,
But, best of all, in our hearts .
There's always tomorrow
To return!

A Lone Parent's Lot

Each one of us is worth four of them.
We are strong and reliable till the end.
Before we share all our assets, and, of course, there's ourselves,
We must trust their motives; they're not just out for themselves.
Be sure they are the genuine thing,
Not the proverbial carrot on a string.
It's only natural one should have doubts,
Fear of being let down and the discouraging shouts
Of "I told you so! He just wants a roof and supplies,
No thoughts for the hurt, the pain and the lies."
Thoughts going through your mind:
'The children need a father figure,
But the washing basket shouldn't need to be bigger.
If only I had a man for heavy DIY.
At least to be there; take the strain when I cry.'
But, we remain strong and diligent till the end.
First things first
Is to find a male ***friend.***

Single Parent

You knew I would do it.
You knew you would win.
I can't cope without you.
You knew I'd cave in.
Problems are still here though.
I'm still feeling useless,
Unwanted, left in limbo,
Desolate and clueless.
Fifteen years a mum.
I still want to resign.
Hand in my notice.
I ***do*** quit this time.
I am insecure, confused and upset.
The only certainty I have is
Regret!

Going Solo

As a single parent it is no joke.
Kids think you're something
At which fun should be poked.
You're the welcoming doormat
They see each and every day,
Wiping their feet as they go on their way.
Lack of respect,
Unless you're determined
To uphold order, routine.
Stand up for yourself.
Fight back for your self-esteem.

Terminally Ill

What with the threat of Aids these days
The need for commitment should make it a craze.
As Freddy Mercury and George Michael once said:
"Too much love can kill you,"
And,
"I'd rather be alone than dead."
It's a deadly serious subject,
Not one to ignore or neglect.
So, "It'll never happen to me,"
Is more of an ostrich philosophy.

No Time Crime

The person who loves you
Will give you their time.
I've no time at all,
So I cannot give mine.
I'm excessively busy,
My life is congested,
Consumed in my children
Where my time's invested.
Share time with them,
You can share life with me,
As simple as that –
No complexity.

The Perfect World

The bond between a husband and wife
Should be made strong for ever,
In the perfect world, just once
And for life.
You know just when
You have found ***the*** right one.
Marriage is not hard work,
It's joyous, more fun!

Life-Watching

Times, places, faces and names,
Words and pictures, feelings and blames,
Thought and touch, sight and sound,
Living and breathing makes the world go round.
Freedom and space, time and energy,
With a will to survive, gives a reason to be.

Television

TV is a powerful thing.
It enters our house, we encourage it in.
Yet, if we didn't like the character of a friend,
The relationship would eventually end.
We lose conversation; kept in a trance-like state.
Docile couch potatoes, tricked into checkmate.
Let's restrict our viewing time,
Wean ourselves away,
Not sit and watch the game of life,
But, ***get out there and play!***

Common Sense

Getting to know me
As well as I need;
As I age with time
I learn life without greed.

With less demands
And no plans ahead,
No dreams to be broken,
No wrong paths to be led.

Whatever is needed,
Whatever is best.
No games to be played,
No need of a test.

I'll do what is right
For the majority concerned.
Less heartache all round,
One lesson I've learnt.

If Only

If, just for once,
You would not lie.
To tell the truth,
Or, at least to try.
I find it hard
To trust you lately,
Even though
I love you greatly.
If only you'd make
One honest move,
A kind gesture,
My doubts to disprove.
Jealousy you caused, applied,
As jealous minds are never satisfied.

Family Tree

Like leaves, we grow from family trees.
Springtime; we're greenly naive.
Summer's a short holiday romance,
It's there and gone like a tender last dance.
When autumn comes, we fade and fall.
Winter, of course, is the end of it all.

Thinking compost is what we amount to,
Remaining green, biodegradable.
We recycle our planet; this wonderful earth,
Returning our shells to the place of their birth.
Authors write for immortality,
Their words still remain,
Though, they no longer be!

Ageing and Broke

I feel like I've cracked a full-length mirror;
Put new shoes on a table; walked under a ladder.
I believed, when you grew up, you could do what you liked –
Stay up much too late, or go out all night.
I never imagined I'd feel so tired;
Be old so quickly, feeling unadmired.
Schooldays must be the best of your life;
You have looks, youth and no financial strife.
Money is the root of all evil, or so they say,
But you can't live without it at the end of the day!

What's a Word?

I'd have told you that I love you,
But you've heard that one before.
Perhaps, I'll never leave you,
A dozen times or more.

There's nothing that can be said,
So something has to be done.
Actions speak more than words,
As your trust, it must be won.

But with all the lines and lies you've heard,
And with all the pain you've endured,
It won't be easy to express to you
Just how much you are adored.

Tell me yourself if you can,
How I can show I am the one?
Time, it's true, will help you re-trust.
I'll inevitably try, as this ***is*** a must.

Cost of Childcare

Don't we have children to share
The responsibility and the care?
Children having to go without,
The other parent cares less, no doubt.

Lack of clothes, food and bedding.
If I'd known back then, I'd have cancelled the wedding.
That's not love for better or worse –
The children never promised that verse –
That is selfish and greedy.
Children deserve much more
Than empty heart and purse,
Not ***living as needy***.

Fear

It was a short walk,
Not unlike any other.
The sky it was dark
With a thick fog for cover.

The path thick with mud,
Not far from my home,
In my own neighbourhood.

It was there that I sensed,
Well aware of a presence
I froze like a rabbit,
Nearing fear I was tense.

He grabbed a hold.
I was losing my will.
With an anxious soul,
His ambition to fulfil.

No hope left for me –
My rape was his thrill.

Dear Diary

As another year is over, I know not what I've achieved,
But only of my emotions a year ago, when I naively believed
That if you kept your head down, worked hard, were honest and true
Then all you ever wished for, would eventually come to you.

As an udder year is over, can't cry over spilt milk. Fortune's a rare-bit,
Use your sense of humour, yoghurt to get on with it!

Silly String

Tackle me, tickle me,
Love me to bits.
Keep me in stiches,
Drive me to fits.
Just make me giggle
Or tickle my toes.
I'll make you laugh simply:
I'll rip off my clothes!

Eternal Sleep

Warm, deep, dark-filled caves,
Your mind afloat in weightlessness
Leaves your carcass in despair,
Sensing depths, still, motionless.

Death is within, awaiting a call.
Do not fear, there's no chill.
Certainty for us all.

Silent not eerie, depths beyond reach.
There in us all
A contentment for each.

Admission to Submission

Every one I thought I could trust
Has let me down.
Why take time to care and believe
If all that I'm left with is the hurt and to grieve?
Self-reliant, I build my wall back up,
We all seem to, that's why the world's mucked up.
I won't let me down,
And even if I do, no one can tell me it's wrong.
I don't know how, or if I can be strong.
Hurt, divorce, hurt, divorce, sad –
It's a pattern I'm following – no good, too bad.
What is the point? I give up, I give in.
Life I have lost,
So I guess that
You win!

Friend to Friend

I'm thinking about you now.
I'm thinking about you all the time.
How we used to be together, inseparable, and you were mine.
I remember those smiles, your frowns,
Your changing moods, your ups, those downs.
Dimply, with moo-cow eyes,
Cheeky smiles, hiding unforgivable lies.
You were just one of those unforgettable people;
A once in a lifetime mate,
Of mind,
Of body,
Of soul.
I'm sorry, ***I thought*** you were great.
Sorry is not weakness, just honest regret.
We were one big mistake
I could never regret!

My Placid Place

Sun glistens through evergreen leaves.
Breeze, so calm, admiring trees.
I laze on the grass, hands behind head
In skin-warming sun – large picnic spread.
Birds bath close by in yesterday's sad weather.
This moment will last – a treasured memory forever.

Thought Less

We don't have much time on this planet.
I'll be blunt, 'cos it just must be said,
By the time we've worked out the rat race,
Why worry? We're like ants, we'll be dead.

Regret

To regret, we must first make a mistake,
Otherwise, it's like an apology before we are late.
People may give us advice to avoid regret,
Though, being human, we've never really learnt yet!
Seeming to think others make the mistakes, which we know are stupid,
But we do the very same thing, being just as avid.
To repeat, where mere mortals fail,
As if sorry is what we wish to hail.
To be left with regret, your heart's at half mast,
We must learn for ourselves, your joy's in the past.

Soul-Lonely, Souled Out

How in a world surrounded by people
Could I ever feel so outcast?
How, only when I try to help,
I receive the majority of the blast?
My soul is tired,
Tired of trying to care.
Showing an interest is taken all wrong.
How I never see, till too late,
I was the sucker all along.
When all I set out to achieve, each and every way,
Is to make at least one person happy each and every day.

Paid in Kind

I had children,
I've paid the price.
I'm ashamed of my body,
I'll admit it's not nice.
I will have to live with me,
Not a pleasant sight in reality.
I gave up bikinis,
Any rights to short tops.
Think twice about babies
Unless you're happy wearing smocks!

My Fond Farewell

It's okay now.
To all those who ever hurt me
I forgive you, it's okay.
To all those who wondered if I loved them,
If I wrote or said so, whenever, then, I did.

To all those I've hurt,
Given choice, I wouldn't have done it first.
To all those I've let down,
It would have been my last option.

To all those who hated me,
You know, love is close to hate.
To all those who liked me,
Thank you, I'd miss you too.

As I take my last rest
In my favourite-place bed,
I'd just like to say,
In every way, it's okay.

Honest Regret

For what I have done wrong, I have regrets
For which I cannot undo,
As much or as many times as I would have liked to.
But to regret, we must firstly do wrong.
We're told of mistakes, avoidable in the long run.
Regret is a feeling you can't give to someone,
Unlike happiness it can so easily be done
By a smile, a simple hug or a kiss,
By phone, let them know just how much they're missed.
So today let how you feel show,
Not too late in the day or tomorrow.
It's up to you to change your fate –
A way to avoid a ***regretful date!***

Soulmate

Falling in love has its reasons,
It's to get people together to breed.
It's then you are inseparable,
Purpose is to germinate the seed.

The vital statistics are sorry to hear,
20% of men want love; 80% want beer.
We always enjoy the practise,
Given the urge was a motive.
What God hadn't counted on
Was invention of contraception.

Two like-minded people
Make one much-wanted soul.
That's, of course, if you're lucky, they say
If the complete family is the goal.

In Your View, Who's Who?

If only you could see with my eyes,
You'd see your transparent disguise.
The quality you have to light up a room,
Before you entered, it was all doom and gloom.

Then you'd see through the macho image,
To the boy seeking his own security.
You'd see the best of the best; the best you can be.
Tell me honestly, how would you see me?

What Goes On?

Oh, just to see inside someone else's head,
To hear what they're thinking, after what's just been said.
Do they really agree, or are they kind and polite?
Are they holding back thought, preventing the fight?
Do they really care?
Or, perhaps there's a motive or plot,
Leading to false security,
To take ***the bloody lot!***

When Love Dies

When the love and friendship dies,
Initially, there's pain, resentment and lies.
After a while we reflect on the joy
Which we see through our children,
Be they girl or be boy.
Love that once glimmered like a shooting star,
Seems just so far, or remains so elusive,
Never recaptured, individually exclusive.
That time of love never seems to last,
It must be grasped, before it's a memory passed!

Dramatic Entrance

What is life, but a staged play.
With no choice to audition,
Forgetting our lines, losing our way,
No wonder!
What parts do we play?

Some men, playing bastard parts,
Say they're loved by women, if they break more hearts.
Some women act easy to please,
When it comes to commitment, they're just a tease.

Some adults playing both Mum and Dad.
The other parents decide to change their own role,
Leaving commitment behind
And signing on the dole.

There is no option, to play your part
Or any choice of what hurts your heart.
But there is an option to help others through
When stage fright hits them, put the spotlight on you.

Let them play the sleeping lion
And have a well-earned rest.
Prove you can be relied upon,
Show them you at your best.

As my character, mentally, physically, I'm damaged goods,
From the hurt inside, to the exterior looks.
I paint on my make-up to hide the fact
My heart and soul are irreparably cracked.

I've avoided eye contact as much as I can,
I've kept my distance from everyone.
Once bitten and my fingers burnt
Too many times, I should have learnt.

I'll play my part, I'll see life through,
But I don't want to come back
If there is a ***Scene Two!***

Positively Mental Tension

It's hold your boobs
As you run down the stairs.
It's bitchy, sarcasm week.
Chocoholism and empty stares.
Feeling you've drunk the contents of a swimming pool.
Wishing to just pull the plug on it all.
Snapping faster than a huffy crocodile.
Out of character, an inch becomes a mile.
Tired, feeling run-down and bloated.
Hair won't go right.
Self-esteem is demoted.

Tub of Lard

Sitting in the bath
I can only but laugh
At the dimples, the wrinkles and flab,
And at ten and a half stone,
Of course I can moan,
'Cos, at five-foot-two, that's bad.

There's a possibility it's middle-age spread,
Though that means by sixty I should be dead.

So what do you do when your body's enormous
And your mind doesn't like that idea?
Keep out that chair, get some exercise there,
And ***stay off my elephant's rear!***

Wake Up to Marriage

Take a look at yourself.
Are you a creature of habit?
Time to spare for each other?
You should reach out and grab it.

Make the most of your lives.
Jointly aim for fair play.
No more negative vibes,
Be ***impulsive some way***.

No Thanks!

Men, men, I've had my fill,
Enough of them, I'm off the pill.

Little boys with cars for toys,
They'll love the kids
But not the noise.

Sport is on TV,
He calls you a bore.
Try a striptease,
He'll snore and ignore.

Except, of course,
When grub is up.
Then he'll sit and wait
Like a worm-ridden pup.

So you stand and wait
For a simple remark.
No thanks at all,
Not even a bark.

No.
No, thanks.
No more men!

That Old Bullshit Charm

You'll find, if your man knows none at all,
Then you feel he doesn't care,
Which, of course, is not the case,
Of that you should be aware.

If he's learnt the art of salesman's patter,
He's probably short of the old grey matter.
Uninteresting, a real old bore,
A two-timing, cheating,
Brainless male whore.

Divorce

Divorce *is* grief.
A solution to a problem.
You believe it will bring relief.

Still you yearn for the end of it all.
The ghost reappears,
No one's there when you call,
Causing never-ending tears.
It reopens the wound.
No time for healing.
You're abandoned, marooned.

It's your heart they're stealing,
You're left lonely and hurt,
Kicked in the teeth,
Left in the dirt.

Life's Battle

Life is a minefield you work your way through.
You must try to guide others,
They could try to help you.

You hear of others
Who've trod on mines,
Leaving the shrapnel in folk left behind.

Much like front line,
Watch out for crossfire
With heat-seeking missiles
To kill off desire.

And just as you're thinking
Life is just fine,
Look out!
Beware!
Are ***you*** stood on a mine?

Euthanasia

Nine out of ten times
There is ***no*** good end.
Killed in a car crash;
Drunk in charge of a friend.

In the Good Book
The saying rings true:
Do unto others
As they do unto you.

Try to relate to unbearable pain,
Even with painkillers
It ***will*** always remain.

Not being able to cope
With the simplest of tasks,
Wishing each breath
Could just be your last.

We all cry out for animal rights,
We kill in wars,
Encourage in fights.

Yet, if it were our family pet
Our concern would remain,
We'd not live and let,
We're sincere and humane.

To help them out gently,
Keep their pride and dignity.
Let us show some respect,
Not just choose to ignore or allow for neglect.

Children

We invent them, resent them,
Love them, hate their mess.
You can even envy them,
For they just do not care less.

You think you know them,
Even show them the error of your ways.
They won't listen, they'll just ask you,
"Were there TVs in your days?"

Innocent, yet knowing,
Just how we need ***showing***
Up in public.

Still we stick to what we do best,
Caring more, instead of less,
'Cos in the end we've made a friend
For life!

Christmas Shopping En-Counter

She set out to get
Herself a brand-new saucepan set.
"Are you sure that is it?"
She announced in despair.
"It's written on the box, madam. It says it just there!"
Her voice grew louder, as customers looked on.
"It says on the computer that's the very last one.
A 3-piece set for boiling and frying.
I promise you, madam, I wouldn't be lying.
Please don't worry about a thing,
It's easy to carry, there's even the string."
She stormed out the shop in complete dismay,
It was then that I spotted it on display.
She was right, I thought to myself in horror,
It ***was*** an empty box that I'd just sold her.

Recipe for Revenge

1: Tie up your victim.

2: Get your hand grenade.

3: Open their mouth.

4: Shove it in.

5: Set up the video.

6: Pull out the pin.

7: Prepare yourself to run like hell,

8: Once the fear sets in.

9: Confirm the smell.

10: Smile and replay the video event.

11: Simmer the victory.

12: No need to stir up, resent.

13: Recipe should be full; complete.

14: If it's correct, revenge will taste sweet.

Unheard Of

From the moment of birth we're traced,
Colour, creed, religion or race.
Registered, tagged, numbered and coded,
Taxed, named, logged and loaded.
Freedom to own a mobile phone –
An electronic tagging all of my own.
Restriction preventing system leave,
Bugged as you talk,
Pay as you breathe.
Freedom, the word, or so it's said,
Has been officially registered and certified ***dead!***

Insane?

A head without a face?
A location with no known place?
Onion peeling makes you laugh?
A bath with no plug, full of water?
Cow's mother a calf?
Dad's son's a daughter?

To not comprehend?
Empty account, spend, spend, spend?
Look with no eyes?
Filling but no pies?
Insane or genius?
Thought or thoughtless,
You think? You know? You guess?
The answer's fail or success?

Boxes

Buy a baby a present and they play more with the box, you'll find.
Even after the age of consent curiosity of the box fascinates their mind.
Be it TV, PC, the latest computer game,
The reaction and addiction are possessing them the same.

Takeaway

Remove the tribal preparing of the feast.
Remove the sharing of the hunted beast.
Make a mess together, clear away as a team.
Disposable dishes, no washing-up to be seen.
Our lives were given us, don't we have a price to pay?
An option to live, take part or takeaway?

Virtually There

Modern human pays bills, works, sleeps.
Fast food, no time to sit down and eat.
Video, PC, TV, Playstation, Nintendo.
Emotions so deep, they seem dormant and shallow.
Virtual husband, creates a real single mum.
Males heading for extinction, nearing the millennium,
Not having to physically interact,
They're virtually there and that's a fact.

Love Potion

You've done nothing but show you care,
Yet, I still test you, you're well aware.
You are determined to prove your devotion
And all I keep doing is causing a commotion.

I'm sorry I haven't stopped feeling hurt,
I'm unable to disguise my emotion.
I know I keep kicking your face in the dirt,
I guess time is the greatest ***love potion***.

Last Verse

Is there ***anything*** I could do or say
That could change your mind in ***any*** way?
Is there ***anything*** I could say or do
To get ***my*** opinion across to ***you***?
Is there anything you would like to ***do***
Or anything you'd care to ***mention***?
Just ***tell me*** what to do or say
To get some ***real*** attention.
I have ***tried*** all I can think of;
I have done ***all*** I can do;
I have one last verse to say
"Goodbye, I ***do*** love you."

Depression or Suppression?

My mum has taken tablets, well over thirty years,
To calm her nerves, numb her pain and suppress all her tears.
Now I am a mum I get that way,
I don't want brain-numbing pills
To see me through the day.
She had electric-shock treatment in her era.
In and out of mental homes, her mind was none the clearer.
It could have just been Pre N D,
Treated very unsuccessfully.
Thirty years on, they've found a cure, we're not insane,
It was a chemical imbalance within the brain.
After a three-month course, I just felt great
Thanks to my mum, but for her it's too late!

Endless Love

Home is where the heart is,
A very well-known line.
What happens if you've lost your heart?
Or your heart is on the line?

Logic is where the mind is,
A not so well-known line.
What happens if you've lost your mind?
Or your mind's not working fine?

Feeling is where the emotion is,
A strange statement, but it's true.
What happens if I lost my emotions?
Do my feelings stop for you?

9 to 5

Scrub up nicely
To tread the well-worn path.
Get through the whole day.
It's continuous graft.

Rush hour first thing
And last thing at night,
In order to improve
Our lifetime of plight.

Walk, drive,
Cycle or bus ride,
Cause to avoid
A financial landslide.

No time at all
To admire the view.
Lunch hour indigestion,
No time to chew.

Paid by the hour
To allow to be restricted,
Individuality,
Freedom destructed.

We are not numbers,
Not ants on a path.
We deserve ***everyday***
To live as our last.

Auntie Mina

Through childhood you were always there,
You taught us love and showed you cared.
Showing patience and kindness,
Not to cry over spilt milk,
Not to be too proud to ask for help.

Not to keep secrets
Or be underhanded,
Keep our feet in our mouths,
If that's how we'd landed.

We'd like to have kept you on a pedestal.
You were a good person
And an example to all.

You were undoubtedly second to none.
We wish we could have called you ***Mum!***

Be Stress Free - Sea

Recipe

1: Float free on rubber ring to size.

2: Await cascades of waves.

3: Release the stress from within.

4: Submit your cares to tides.

5: Wash away worries.

6: Release your control.

7: Abandon financial strife.

8: Cleanse your soul.

9: Disregard others.

10: Embrace a whole new life!

The Big 4 0

Reverse the butterfly stage,
Say goodbye to your looks.
Hello, caterpillar –
Middle age!

You could fly before,
Now you're down to a crawl.
Extra rolls of body,
Not slim and beautiful.

Taking longer, trying harder
To turn over the new leaf.
Your body betrays you,
Your mind becomes a thief.

Seek a slower pace.
Ferris wheel of seasons.
Why I did half I did?
I'm now unable to see reasons.

Life begins,
So they say.
What kind of life
At the end of the day?

Circle of Anxiety

Why worry?
Analyse – processing "Why"

No answer.

What's the problem?
Analyse – processing "What"

Answer – There is no specific problem.

When did I begin to feel this way?
Analyse – processing "When"

I'm becoming forgetful – Answer – I don't know.

Where did my memory go?
Analyse – processing "Where"

Answer – What's the question again?

Who do I turn to?
Analyse – processing "Who"

Answer – Me.
Why worry?

Daisy's Field

What is a view to you
Means the world to me,
Golden memories of old.
Picture the scene as the years unfold,
Once like mere bushes, aligning a bank,
A heaven aspiring avenue, thanks to my brother, Frank.
And the tall stone chimney, that peers from behind,
Brings thoughts of Grandfather, forefront in my mind.

The miracle of ponies bearing foals.
Cascading balloons, like a giant game of bowls.
Spring-water floods; a field of tears.
At 5 a.m. a lonesome deer.
The pasture's not mine
But the view ***is*** my own.
It means so much to me,
This place ***is*** my home.

Depression

Emotionally destitute,
Stripped naked,
No 'Confidence suit'.

In the raw,
Surrounded, exposed,
Amongst the crowd,
Stood, but dozed.

Caught up in the gossip of life,
Unable to speak.
To be heard,
They so desperately seek.

Heartache is history,
Now it's bleeding and raw.
Take time to listen,
Not just show them the door.

Five minutes is all it may take
To hear, acknowledge,
And clarify a mistake.

Time for each other these days
Is so rare,
Think twice!
Do you ***really*** have time to spare?

The world could be a better place
If we'd slow down to care
For the humankind ***race.***

Examine the Exams

Measure of the mind?
Years of force-feeding
But do unchewed facts bind?

How well we regurgitate
Calibrates our capacity
For future meal intake.

Who decides when?
You yourself are full.
Is it up to you
To take one more spoonful?

Will it make you sick?
Become too much?
No one else has the right
To tell you to digest as such.

More facts to fill yourself with,
Leaving less brain capacity
For emotions, common sense.
A bookworm
Can get worms you see!

Heaven Scent

Like John in my heart, my beech tree
Takes pride of place.
Brought home as a seedling,
Vibrant green with leafy lace.

Wind batters the foliage about,
People comment, "It's late coming out."
Carpeted lawn, hedged honeysuckle
And golden leylandii smells so wonderful.

Scented broom and daphne o-dora,
Fragrant wisteria, sadly over.
Charles is stood neath the glory of our tree,
Amidst nature's perfume, lily of the valley.

Sweet peas entwine a bamboo steeple,
Wallflower's departed, like much-loved people.
I'll never tire of looking down –
My own piece of England –
My jewel in the crown.

Life in Order

Routinely I get up.
Routinely I arise.
Routinely put on make-up
On routinely tired eyes.

Routinely I get washed.
Routinely I get dressed.
Routinely eat my breakfast.
I'm routinely so hard-pressed.

Routinely I do housework.
Routinely shop for food.
Routinely I say, "Good morning,"
As routinely I'm not rude.

Routinely I dream
Routinely of less strife.
Routinely I got married;
I'm a routine mum and wife.

Routinely I'll look back.
Routinely old and grey.
Routinely I will say,
"Oh, how I miss the good old days!"

Loud and Proud

Antony, Samantha, Steven and Jon,
I'm proud to say, "I am their mum."
I love them with all my heart and soul,
My children,
My babies,
My gold!

They truly are my only treasures
And brought me untold
Grief and pleasures.

Real characters and individually strong,
I'm proud to say,
"I am their mum."

Mother's Love

A mother's love is boundless
And limitless, it's true.
I love my children endlessly.
My babies, "I love you."

With all my thoughts and imperfections,
Regrets, mistakes I've made.
You've loved me too, no matter what,
You've turned out how I'd prayed.

When I'm no longer here to tell you,
Keep me in your heart,
I'll love you still.
We share a bond
No one call tear apart.

Office Blues

Clean, tidy, neat, polite,
Leave home early,
Proverbial bomb site.

Put aside family ties,
Separate worries,
Keep them disguised.

Rent yourself out,
A few pounds per hour,
Sweet smile hides the sour.

Lunch hour,
Your time to be free
Or at least it's supposed to be.

Back to the grindstone,
Imprisoned,
Busy, no time to moan.

Half an hour to go,
I daydream
Through an open window.

Arrive and clear the bomb site,
Prepare a meal,
Settle for the night.

Then, before bed,
Get ready
For another day of ***dread!***

Proportion Abortion

You were caught,
I was red-handed.
A 'Murderer,'
I had self-branded.

Blood on my hands.
A decision I made
For your life
In the palm of my hands.

I allowed them to kill you,
Dissect with their blades.
Painful-day memories,
The guilt never fades.

Every year a birthday
Regurgitates the pain
Of what would have been
Had I let you remain.

As Burt Reynolds
Agreeably said:
"It's a sin I will carry
Until I am dead."

Teenage Inrage

Don't listen to me, I know nothing.
Don't tidy your room.
Don't forget I am a cash machine; taxi service.
I love to cook and clean. I'm at one with my broom.

You are ***never*** too much trouble.
You're the last thing on my mind.
When I tell you something
I'm just aiming to be unkind.

Drama queen's upon her throne,
Thrown to one side, abandoned, alone.
Let me be there to listen to your woe
So you can tell me where to go!

Snakes and Ladders of Life

Begin the game.
Enthusiasm and zest.
All can be achieved.
You're going to be the best.

Hit the first ladder,
Keen to climb.
Life can't be better
Here up on cloud nine.

Your job's at risk,
Comes a close call.
Encounter a snake,
It's okay, you don't fall.

Lucky go.
Ladder to climb.
Plenty more goes.
Took a career path
And successfully rose.

Threw a one,
Steeped back two.
A little snake;
I had the flu.

I'm heading towards
My biggest chance
I threw a six,
Means great advance.

Lose a turn.
I throw a double.
Larger snake
Could mean trouble.

Wow! I can't believe
My good fortune.
The longest ladder –
Is this promotion?

My goal's in sight,
A winner in life.
Too good to be true,
I'll be free from strife.

My cup overflows;
Not how I expect.
The board's wet and soggy –
Spilt milk – no regret.

Tidy-ness-cesity

So what if my hair's a mess?
It's clean, no nits,
A sign of genius!

Einstein did not have a tidy mop!
As a man, they never demanded
He brush his hair or crop!

Allow me to express.
I thought this hair was mine.
Women that don't nit-pick?
Not in my lifetime!

Victim

Play the victim,
Act the part,
Cheat yourself
Of strength of heart.

Hold your head down,
Admit defeat,
Confirm the labels,
Invoice the receipt.

What would a friend say
If you told them your blues?

Be your own best friend
Or a victim –
You choose!

What If?

What if I hadn't met you?
What if we'd never spoke?

What if you hadn't noticed me,
My what if only, bloke?

I wouldn't have sweet memories
That make me smile within.

I wouldn't know what I had missed,
Your (for my eyes only) grin.

We were together for a reason,
We never had a tiff.

The reason's becoming clear to me,
I need to dream
What if?